Our Guests

Our Guests

Our Guests

Our Guests

Our Guests

Our Guests

Our Guests

Our Guests

Our Guests

Our Guests

Our Guests

Our Guests

Our Guests

Our Guests

Our Guests

Our Guests

Our Guests

Our Guests

Our Guests

Our Guests

Our Guests

Our Guests

Our Guests

Our Guests

Our Guests

Our Guests

Our Guests

Our Guests